Roberta Bondar

Leading Science into Space

MICHAEL WEBB

Copp Clark Pitman Ltd.
A Longman Company

ISBN 0-7730-5288-7

Canadian Cataloguing in Publication Data
Webb, Michael, 1949–
      Roberta Bondar, leading science into space

(Scientists and inventors series) Includes index.
ISBN 0-7730-5288-7

1. Bondar, R.L. (Roberta L.), 1945–   - Juvenile literature. 2. Astronauts - Canada - Biography - Juvenile literature. I. Title. II. Series: Scientists and inventors series.

TL789.85.B66W42 1993   j629.45'0092   C92-095400-6

MICHAEL WEBB, a former school teacher and chemistry professor, now works as an editor and writer in Toronto. He has a doctorate in chemistry from the University of Alberta.

EDITING AND PHOTO RESEARCH: *Grace D'Alfonso*
SERIES DESIGN: *Susan Hedley*
ART DIRECTION AND LAYOUT: *Kyle Gell*
PRINTING AND BINDING: *Friesen Printers Ltd.*

ACKNOWLEDGMENTS
Many thanks to Dr. Roberta Bondar for reading and commenting on the manuscript. Also, special thanks to Ryan Croft, aged 9, and Adel Raso, aged 12, for reading the manuscript.

PHOTO AND ILLUSTRATION CREDITS
Canada Post Corporation: 1; Canadian Space Agency: cover, iv, 10, 11, 12, 14; Canapress: 15, 25; McLaughlin Planetarium: 2; McMaster University, Faculty of Health Sciences: 6; NASA: 7, 8, 9, 13, 16, 17, 18, 19, 20, 21, 22, 23; Ontario Ministry of Natural Resources: 5; *The Sault Star:* 3, 4; Toronto Star Syndicate: 24.

Copp Clark Pitman Ltd.
2775 Matheson Blvd. East
Mississauga, Ontario L4W 4P7

Printed and bound in Canada.

  3 4 5 5288-7 00 99 98

CONTENTS

Dr. Roberta Bondar.

INTRODUCTION

The great challenge of the first space flights was to launch the rocket without an accident. When the first astronauts went into space, the main aims were to keep them alive there and to bring them back safely.

Though space flight is still dangerous, it has moved into a new stage. Top scientists are going into space to find out if humans can live there for a long time. One of these scientists is Dr. Roberta Bondar. In January, 1992, she became the second Canadian to fly in space.

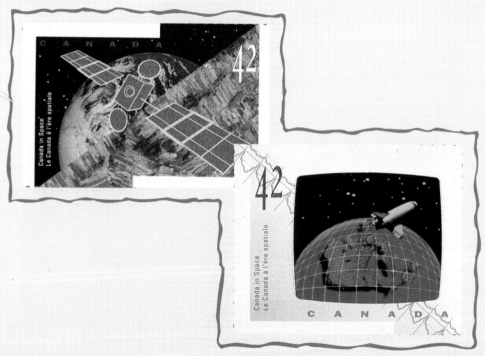

These stamps honour Canada's achievements in space.

CHILDHOOD

Roberta Lynn Bondar was born in Sault Ste. Marie, Ontario, on December 4, 1945. She grew up in a very close family with her older sister, Barbara. The girls' mother, Mildred, was a school teacher. Their father, Edward, worked for the city. Roberta's family loved camping and the outdoors. The girls learned to ski, skate, canoe, and play all kinds of other sports.

When Roberta was in grade 7, her father built her a **laboratory** in the basement of the house. Roberta did experiments with test tubes supplied by her father. She also used a microscope that was a gift from her Uncle Arthur, who was a **pharmacist**.

The Northern Lights.

Can you find 16-year-old Roberta in this class photo?

As early as age eight, Roberta was thinking about space. She watched the **Northern Lights** and the stars. She read science fiction books and watched science fiction movies on TV. Roberta imagined being part of the stories.

When Roberta was a teenager, her Aunt Erma was working in Florida and sending her news of the American space program. The walls of Roberta's bedroom were covered in posters about space. Roberta liked to build models of rockets and tried to watch **satellites** going overhead at night.

She already knew that there were three things she wanted to be — a medical doctor, a scientist, and an astronaut.

THE YOUNG SCIENTIST

Roberta was "female athlete of the year."

Roberta did not only like science and space. She was a Girl Guide and was very keen on sports. She led camping and canoe trips, and coached sports at the YMCA. Basketball was one of her favourites. She was "female athlete of the year" in her last year of high school.

In high school, Roberta overcame her dislike of insects by studying tent caterpillars for a science fair. Her project won second prize. Even better, it led to summer jobs doing **research** for the Department of Fisheries and Forestry in Sault Ste. Marie. She did research on the spruce budworm, which feeds on Canadian trees.

Roberta studied **zoology** and **agriculture** at the University of Guelph. She went back to her research job in the summers. She also found time to coach the university **archery** team and to learn to fly a single-engine plane. In 1968, she graduated from Guelph and got her pilot's license.

Roberta moved on to the University of Western Ontario and the University of Toronto. In 1974, she completed her **doctorate** in Toronto. Her research was in **neurology**. She studied how the brains of goldfish are affected by the temperature of the water they live in.

Next came medical school at McMaster University in Hamilton, Ontario. She became a medical doctor in 1977. After 13 years of study and research, she had achieved two of her three career goals. At age 31, she was Dr. Roberta Bondar, a scientist and medical doctor. But there was no sign that she would ever go into space.

Tent caterpillars.   *Spruce budworms.*

BUILDING A CAREER

Dr. Bondar worked at Toronto General Hospital, then at the University of Western Ontario. In 1981, she headed for Tuft's New England Medical Centre in Boston, before returning to Toronto to work at Toronto Western Hospital.

In 1982, her career took a big step forward. Dr. Bondar became an assistant professor of medicine at McMaster University. She also became the director of a clinic that treated people with **multiple sclerosis**.

The Health Sciences Centre Building at McMaster University.

An American astronaut on the moon.

Dr. Bondar wrote articles about her research. In one of them, she described a heart problem that might cause a child to have a **stroke**.

Dr. Bondar still thought about space. There had been many developments since she was a child. The first astronaut, Yuri Gagarin from Russia, had flown over 20 years earlier, on April 12, 1961. The American space program, run by the National Aeronautics and Space Administration (NASA), had sent many astronauts into space. The best-known flight had landed American astronauts on the moon on July 20, 1969.

THE SPACE SHUTTLE

Early astronauts were rescued after their capsule splashed into the ocean.

NASA began its space shuttle program in 1972. The shuttle would carry more people and heavier loads than earlier rockets. It would also fly back to Earth, so that it could be used over and over. Earlier rockets had only been used once. Astronauts had returned to the Earth by floating down in a small **capsule** hanging from a parachute. They splashed into the ocean, where ships were waiting to pick them up.

By 1977, shuttle test flights had begun. The **prototype** shuttle, *Enterprise*, was launched from the back of a Boeing 747, so that the shuttle pilot could practise landing. When a shuttle returns to the Earth, it has no fuel and must glide down. The pilot gets only one chance to land safely.

A Canadian company, Spar Aerospace Limited, developed the Canadarm for the space shuttle. This robot arm is about 15 m long. It lifts large objects, such as satellites, in and out of the shuttle's **cargo bay**, while the shuttle is in space.

On April 12, 1981, exactly 20 years after the first astronaut had flown in space, the shuttle *Columbia* made its first space flight. By the end of 1985, three other shuttles, *Challenger, Discovery*, and *Atlantis*, had also flown.

NASA wanted scientists to fly on the shuttles. NASA called these scientists "payload specialists." Their job was to do experiments, not to work as pilots. In 1983, Dr. Ulf Merbold of Germany became the first non-American to fly on the shuttle as a payload specialist. On his flight, the shuttle *Columbia* carried *Spacelab* for the first time. This laboratory fits into the shuttle's cargo bay.

The Canadarm.

THE CANADIAN ASTRONAUTS

In Ottawa, the National Research Council of Canada (NRC) set up the Canadian Astronaut Program in 1983. In July, the NRC advertised for payload specialists. Dr. Bondar applied right away. She felt the advertisement "called out loud and clear: 'Roberta Bondar, where are you?'"

Over 4300 other people applied! It took six months of paperwork, interviews, and health tests for the NRC to choose six astronauts. Dr. Bondar had great news on the day before her thirty-eighth birthday. She was in the astronaut program! She hoped to be in space within two or three years.

In March, 1984, it was announced that Dr. Marc Garneau would be the first Canadian in space. His **backup** was Dr. Bob Thirsk. But all six astronauts began training. They trained in Canada, and at NASA centres in Texas and Florida.

The Canadian astronauts.

A difficult part of the training dealt with space sickness. Many astronauts had been sick in space. The astronauts were tested in spinning and tumbling machines to see if they were likely to get sick.

Marc Garneau and Bob Thirsk practised on NASA's training plane, the KC-135. This plane climbs and dives very steeply. As it stops climbing and starts to dive, passengers feel **weightless** for about 20 seconds. They can float around and bounce off of the padded walls to get used to being weightless, as they will be in space.

Dr. Marc Garneau training in a spinning chair.

Astronauts during a KC-135 training flight.

SUCCESS AND FAILURE

On October 5, 1984, Dr. Garneau became the first Canadian in space. He was one of the crew of seven on the shuttle *Challenger*. Dr. Bondar watched the launch and gave a live TV commentary.

Dr. Garneau was back eight days later, after circling the Earth 132 times. He travelled almost 5 500 000 kilometres (over 14 times the distance from the Earth to the moon)! When he landed, Dr. Bondar was one of the scientists who tested him to find out the effects of the trip on his body.

Though Dr. Garneau was a Canadian hero, the future was not clear for the other astronauts. Over a year later, the NRC chose Dr. Steve MacLean as the next Canadian in space. Bjarni Tryggvason was his backup. But then came a terrible accident.

Dr. Marc Garneau in space.

The shuttle Challenger *blew up.*

On January 28, 1986, just 73 seconds after liftoff, seven astronauts died when the *Challenger* blew up. Dr. Bondar still wanted to fly in space, but no one knew when that might happen. She might never fly at all.

She carried on training and managed to do some research. In 1988, Dr. Bondar joined the staff at Sunnybrook Medical Centre in Toronto. She did experiments on NASA's KC-135 aircraft to measure the blood flow to the brain during weightlessness.

Dr. Bondar's research will help scientists to understand some changes that happen to astronauts in space. It may also help doctors to deal with medical problems on Earth, such as how to treat stroke victims.

Waiting and Training

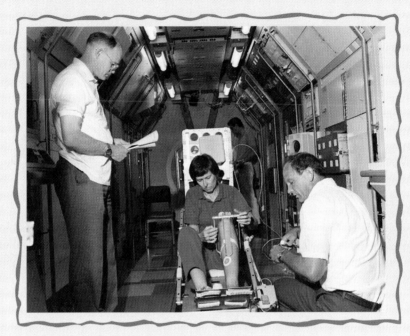

Training for IML-1.

When shuttles began flying again in 1989, Canada was already planning for more flights. Dr. Bondar and Dr. Ken Money were travelling to meetings with 200 scientists. Their experiments would be done in *Spacelab* on the first International Microgravity Laboratory mission (IML-1). The scientists voted for the person they wanted to do their experiments. They chose Dr. Bondar.

On January 20, 1990, Canadian newspapers announced that Dr. Roberta Bondar would be the next Canadian astronaut! Dr. Money would be her backup. Her flight had been moved ahead of Steve MacLean's.

Dr. Bondar trained even harder. She was flying between NASA bases in Texas and Alabama every few days. In a typical day, she would get up around 6:00 a.m., exercise for an hour, then work for 12 to 14 hours. She was so busy that she carried a bag of snacks around, in case there was no time for meals.

She practised experiments over and over. In space, she would only have one chance to get them right. She also practised escaping from an accident, such as a crash into the ocean. Dr. Bondar learned to **scuba dive** to get used to surviving in the water. She had very little free time for flying aircraft, which she loved, but she found time for some hot air ballooning.

A scuba diver.

LIFTOFF!

Dr. Bondar's flight was set for December 6, 1990, but the shuttles had fuel leaks. In fact, Dr. Bondar's flight was delayed by over a year. She had to wait until January 22, 1992, for the greatest moment of her life.

This time, there was a delay of only an hour as she waited in the shuttle *Discovery* with the six other crew members. Then they were off.

The launch was the most dangerous time, and the seven astronauts cheered when the two largest rockets fell away two minutes into the flight. Dr. Bondar was safely on her way.

Discovery *lifts off.*

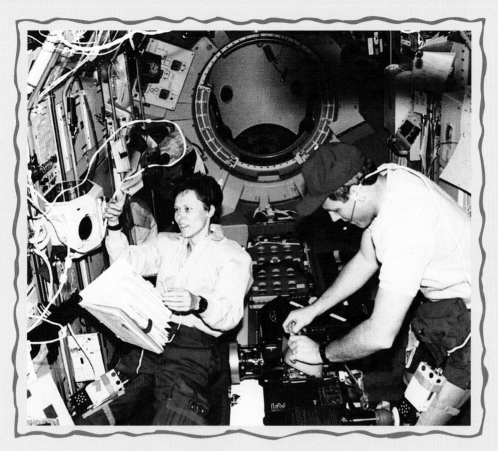

Working in Spacelab.

Only nine minutes after liftoff, the shuttle was in orbit about 300 kilometres above the Earth (the distance from Edmonton to Calgary). About three hours into the flight, Dr. Bondar floated into *Spacelab* and started her experiments.

She was one of two payload specialists. The other was Dr. Ulf Merbold, the German who had flown in *Spacelab* nine years earlier. They each worked twelve hours a day, so the experiments never stopped.

LIVING IN SPACE

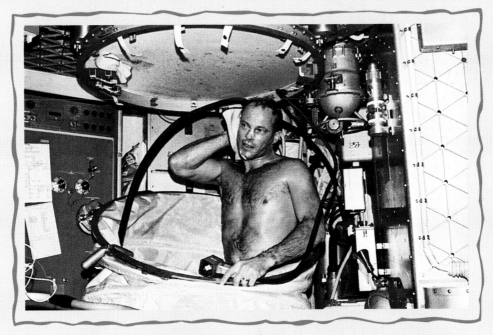

An astronaut washing in space.

Each astronaut had to help clean the shuttle and make meals. There is no refrigerator on a shuttle. Most of the food is dried, so water must be added to it. Dr. Bondar found that a lot of the food did not have much taste. She took along some food of her own, including some Girl Guide cookies. But she lost three kilograms on the flight.

Because of the low **gravity**, eating could be a challenge. Food could float away. Dr. Bondar described how: "Sometimes, you could be minding your own business, eating something, and suddenly this ball of someone else's food comes and it just sticks on the side of your eye, and then SPLAT — right on your eyeball."

Washing, dressing, and using the toilet are all much harder and take longer in space. And sleeping is really different. Straps held Dr. Bondar in her "sleep cabinet," to stop her from floating away. Her head was held onto the pillow with Velcro!

There was not much time to relax. Dr. Bondar had some of her favourite music tapes with her. She also spent a little time looking at the Earth. The shuttle even passed over her home in Northern Ontario. She decided that: "There is no boring place anywhere on this whole planet."

A view of the Earth from space.

EXPERIMENTS

Dr. Bondar did dozens of experiments. Some of them studied how the human body changes in space. She helped to measure her own back and the backs of other astronauts to see how their shapes changed. Most astronauts have back pains and get taller in space. Dr. Bondar grew by five centimetres. By studying back pains in space, doctors hope to help people with back problems on Earth.

The astronauts tested their sense of direction in space. They pointed a light at five targets after looking at them and closing their eyes.

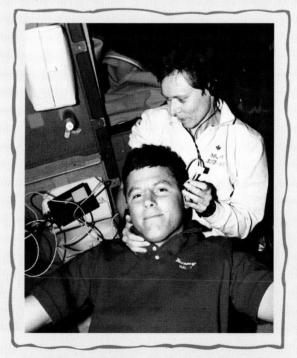

Dr. Bondar checking another astronaut in space.

A camera in this helmet recorded eye movements.

An experiment that studied balance and space sickness had Dr. Bondar spinning in a chair. She wore a helmet with a camera inside to follow the motion of her eyes. Dr. Bondar also tested her **reflexes** and balance on a small sled fixed to the floor. The sled could move back and forth a short distance along the floor.

There were experiments with small living things, such as frog **embryos**. To grow food, space travellers will need to know how plants grow in space. Dr. Bondar studied the growth of oats, wheat, and other plants.

Dr. Bondar also grew **crystals**. They grow much larger in space than on Earth. We may one day grow crystals of useful drugs much more easily in space than on Earth.

BACK TO EARTH

The Discovery *crew for IML-1.*

Humans lose **body fluids** in space. Just before returning to Earth, the astronauts took salt pills and a drink of water. They also put anti-gravity suits on their legs, to push blood up to the heart and brain. Otherwise, as gravity pulls more blood into the legs, astronauts may feel dizzy or faint.

Like all astronauts, Dr. Bondar had a puffy face in space. The liquid that gravity usually holds in the legs spreads around the body. The extra liquid in the face makes it puffy. Dr. Bondar's eyesight also changed. She had shopped for a new pair of glasses before her flight, but she did not need them in space. No one knows why.

Dr. Bondar landed safely in California on January 30, 1992. Being back on Earth was not easy. Astronauts feel very heavy after they land. Dr. Bondar said that "it was like we had bowling balls for heads."

After she landed, there were eleven days of tests to check the effects of the flight. Her puffiness soon went, and she needed her glasses again. Her height also went back to normal.

A safe landing.

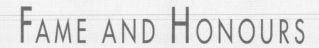

FAME AND HONOURS

As soon as she had time, Dr. Bondar went home. The welcome in Sault Ste. Marie on February 19, 1992, was incredible. Hundreds of people met her at the airport, and thousands crowded a stadium to see her. The city now has a park and a government building named after her.

As Dr. Bondar leaves the astronaut program in 1992, she already has many awards for her work. These include twelve **honorary degrees** from Canadian universities. In 1992, she received a great honour from her country. She was named an Officer of the Order of Canada for her "achievement...of a high degree." No more than 46 Canadians are given this award in any year.

A hero's welcome in Sault Ste. Marie.

Dr. Bondar receiving an honorary degree at the University of Toronto.

On March 23, 1992, the Government of Ontario announced the Roberta Bondar Science and Technology Education Awards Program. Its aim is to get more young people to become scientists.

Though she already has many great achievements, Dr. Bondar still has much of her career ahead of her. Whatever she does in the future, this outstanding Canadian will no doubt apply her limitless energy and her will to succeed. Dr. Bondar describes herself as an "organized tornado." It is hard to disagree.

GLOSSARY

agriculture – Farming. *(p. 5)*

archery – Using a bow to shoot arrows at a target. *(p. 5)*

backup – A person who can take over if needed. *(p. 10)*

body fluids – Liquids inside the body. *(p. 22)*

capsule – A small cabin carried into space by a rocket. *(p. 8)*

cargo bay – A storage section on the outside of the shuttle. *(p. 9)*

crystals – Glittery chunks. (Table salt, sugar, and diamonds are examples of crystals.) *(p. 21)*

doctorate – The highest degree a person can study for in a university. A person working for a doctorate does **research**. *(p. 5)*

embryos – Young animals before they are born. *(p. 21)*

gravity – The pull of one object on another. (The pull of the Earth stops us from floating away.) *(p. 18)*

honorary degrees – A special type of **doctorate** a university can give. An honorary degree rewards a person for good work in the arts, sciences, business, or some other field. *(p. 24)*

laboratory – A room where scientists do experiments. *(p. 2)*

multiple sclerosis – A disease of the brain and spine. *(p. 6)*

neurology – The study of the human nervous system and its diseases. The nervous system includes the brain, spine, and parts of the skin, eyes, ears, nose, and tongue. *(p. 5)*

Northern Lights – Natural light sometimes seen in the northern sky at night. *(p. 3)*

pharmacist – A person who makes or sells medicines. (Every drug store has at least one pharmacist.) *(p. 2)*

prototype – The first example of something new, such as a new kind of car or airplane. The makers build and test a prototype to make sure that it works well. *(p. 8)*

reflexes – Movements that you cannot control. (Shivering in the cold and "jumping" when you hear a loud bang are examples of reflexes.) *(p. 21)*

research – Work done to find out and explain new facts. *(p. 4)*

satellites – Objects that orbit a planet. Many satellites built by people now orbit the Earth. *(p. 3)*

scuba dive – Go underwater with a tank of air on your back, so that you can breathe. *(p. 15)*

stroke – An injury to the brain caused by a broken or blocked blood vessel. (A blood vessel is a tube that carries blood around the body.) *(p. 7)*

weightless – Not feeling any **gravity**. *(p. 11)*

zoology – The scientific study of animals. *(p. 5)*

Index